Federico Nicolaci

Patterns
of Disintegration
The EU and the Emerging
European Order

EUROPEAN REFORM INITIATIVE PRESS

EUROPEAN REFORM INITIATIVE PRESS

Copyright © 2012 by Federico Nicolaci

ISBN 978-1479121557
ISBN 147912155X

Und ferne lausch ich hin, ob nicht ein

Freundlicher Retter vielleicht mir komme.

Friedrich Hölderlin

CONTENTS

Acknowledgments p. 9

PART 1 FRAMING THE EU CRISIS

1 Introduction p.15

2 From Self-congratulation to disintegration p. 23

PART 2 FINDING THE ORIGIN OF EU'S DISINTEGRATIVE DYNAMICS p. 29

3 History: strategic necessity of European integration p.31

4 Functionalism as philosophy of integration: blending pragmatism and idealism p.37

PART 3 THE EU OR THE TRIUMPH OF SUBSTANCIAL VACUITY

5 The End of the Cold War and the beginning of the disintegration of Europe p.41

6 Patterns of disintegration unveiled p.45

7 Monetary (dis)union p.47

8 Enlargement and political (dis)union p.53

9 The Emerging European Order p.59

10 On the European society and the identity of the EU p.65

CONCLUSION: WAKE-UP, EUROPE! p.73

Bibliography p.77

Notes p. 81

Acknowledgments

THE CORE of this essay was written at the end of a period of study at the London School of Economics, and owes much to the inspiring teaching I received from a variety of people. In particular, I would like to express my gratitude to Spyros Economides, Maurice Fraser and Bob Hancké for having enhanced and refined, with their art, my comprehension of that multifaceted entity which is contemporary Europe.

The timing for an essay on the disintegrative dynamics of Europe could not be more appropriate. Indeed, whilst the crisis of Europe intensifies, the political debate at EU level continues to focus on short-term problems and immediate remedies. Europe is a vessel that is sinking and where everyone is working busy to boost the power of the engines and make the cruise more confortable. EU leaders talk about the 'necessity' to move towards a banking and fiscal union, but few of them seem to consider that *the problem* of the European Union might reside in its *ideological* architecture. To be sure, a technical approach to the crisis is resulting in technical and impromptu solutions, deferring the healthy exercise of a philosophical and historical enquiry into the origin of the centrifugal forces that, come in the house of Europe 'like a thief in the night', are posing an existential threat to the EU. Despite my debt to many, all mistakes are mine alone.

F. N.

Venezia, August 2012

Hamlet: Are you honest?

Ophelia: My lord?

Hamlet: Are you fair?

Ophelia: What means your lordship?

Hamlet: That if you be honest and fair – your honesty should admit no discourse to your beauty.

Ophelia: Could beauty, my lord, have better commerce

than with honesty?

Hamlet: Ay, truly. For the power of beauty will sooner transform honesty from what it is to a bawd, than the force of honesty can translate beauty into his likeness.

W. Shakespeare, "Hamlet", III. I.

Patterns of Disintegration

The EU and the Emerging European Order

An Essay by

Federico Nicolaci

PART 1

Framing the crisis of the European Union

1 Introduction: phenomenology of disintegration

"If we look to European Union as a catch-all solution, chanting 'Europe' like a mantra and waving the banners of 'Europe' in the face of recalcitrant 'nationalist' heretics, we may wake up one day to find that far from solving the problems of our continent, the myth of 'Europe' has become an impediment to recognizing them".

Tony Judt

PARAPHRASING MARX, one could say that a spectre is hunting Europe -the spectre of disintegration. Navigating the stormy waters of the global financial crisis, the flagship of the European integration process, namely the European Monetary Union, has revealed all its contradictions and structural flaws. As the euro risks sinking, policymakers in Europe prop up the leaky compartments, but the vessel's structural, architectonical problems are not being addressed. Evidently, the financial tampons adopted by the European Union (EU) leaders can cure the symptoms, but not the cause; and the fundamental cause of the Monetary Union's crisis is not to be found in the 'holy' temple of economics, but in the mundane realm of politics[i]. Indeed, the crisis of the European Monetary Union, which in the intentions of its creators had to be both the *cherry* on the cake of the single market and the *seed* of further political integration, seems to call into question the core assumption of more than half a century of European integration history: the (functionalist) idea that economic integration would be self-sustaining and would ultimately lead to the emergence of a political community[ii].

The thesis of the essay is that, despite the high degree of *legalist* or *formal* integration achieved, 'Europe' at the beginning of the 2010s is internally characterised by powerful disintegrative tendencies. I argue that these centrifugal tendencies are the result of two factors: the end of the Cold War and a tragically incomplete method of integration, which assumed a spillover-driven integration process based on material cooperation. Born as a crucial piece of the international order institutionalized by the United States after the Second World War, the EU is today a hybrid entity daughter of historical circumstances and ideological ambiguity. The end of the Cold War represented a major historical discontinuity for both the United States and Europe, for it entailed the 'exhaustion' of the Western European bloc as a strategic necessity to contain the Soviet Union: the changed strategic landscape offered to Europe the possibility to develop an autonomous political project of integration.

I will argue that two circumstances hindered the development of a coherent project of political integration: first, the American unwillingness to lose the monopoly of the Western security, exercised through NATO, even *after* the end of the Cold War; second, the inability of the member states to transcend and reconcile their national interests in a grand political project of European integration. Notwithstanding the *political* nature behind the 'choice for Europe', the European leaders did not seriously recalibrate the project on the basis of the changed political landscape in the 1990s[iii]. Thus, in spite of some timid attempts to move towards the establishment of a truly political community, the approach to integration after the Cold War remained largely technocratic and functionalist: Europe proved "unable to spell out the very purpose of European integration and of its own existence"[iv]. Integration was not guided by a clear and shared political vision, but by the imperative of expanding the single market[v]; enlargement was not about the definition of Europe's strategic purpose, but about Europe's transformative power, a mere technical exercise of institutional engineering[vi]. The lack of consensus about the meaning and the scope of integration is clearly reflected in the vagueness of the Lisbon Treaty, according to which the Union's aim is that of promoting "peace, its values and the well-being of its people"[vii]. The commitment to such undisputable as well as empty principles is the mask of unresolved disputes about the meaning of integration, and today's EU flawed design is the product of such latent ambiguities and deep controversies.

Paradoxically, the lack of a political approach to integration has fostered the emergence of centrifugal forces (rising nationalism, mutual distrust and lack of cohesion *in primis*), which have alienated public support, thereby severely threatening the fortunes of the EU project[viii]. The failure of the 'Constitution for Europe', the 2010 deadly riots in the street of Athens, divergent national geopolitical interests and the reciprocal mistrust between the peoples of Europe unveiled by the financial crisis indicate that more than half a century of *functional* integration has not unified the peoples of Europe.

Today, the integration of Europe has reached a stall situation, as any step forward seems politically unattainable, but any step back historically unconceivable. The process of functional integration has thus led the train of Europe to a blind track. Somewhere in-between fully national sovereignty and fully political integration, the EU is proving unable to govern the political and economic dynamics of our time –and to solve its own crisis. Indeed, 'halfway integration', whereby member states are autonomous in some policy areas, but subject to supranational authority in other, is proving unstable[ix]. Powerful member states are redrawing their strategic policies, often using the formal framework of the EU as a fig leaf of their national interests, thereby emptying the European Union of all political meaning. As a report produced by the European Council on Foreign Relations (ECFR) suggests, the 'engine of Europe', Germany, continues to officially declare support to the European cause, but is *de facto* rapidly scaling down its commitment to Europe. "The primacy that Europe once assumed in German foreign policy has gone. Berlin now coolly calculates the costs of integration and views its European future with unromantic sobriety. Nobody there still seems to believe in the idea of "ever closer union"[x].

The EU fragmented and segmented decision-making process, the lack of internal coordination and the general predominance of national interests are undermining the ability of the EU to effectively meet the economic, political and geo-strategic challenges of the 21st century as they evolve. On present trends, the American National Intelligence Council believes that Europe "will be losing clout in 2025, while the EU will likely remain a hobbled giant, distracted by *internal* bickering and *competing* national agendas"[xi]. As noted by Paul Taylor, the risk for the EU to become hardly more than a 'high authority' for the management of the single market or an ordinary international organization is more than a pessimistic speculation[xii].

The essay is structured as follows. First, it indicates that, in spite of the widespread optimism associated with the introduction of the Euro and enlargement, signs of contradiction between the rhetoric of a 'closer Union' and the reality of a divided Europe emerged in the early 2000s. As official speeches and our interviews indicate, *idéologues* in the European Commission nourished, and continue to nourish, a shortsighted faith in the ability of the functional logic of integration to unite Europe. I argue that the reciprocal mistrust and tension between the peoples of Europe unveiled by the crisis seems to falsify the expectations of the Commission and corroborate the realist hypothesis that economic integration can at most mask, but no cure, political and nationalistic frictions.

The second part investigates the historical and philosophical *origins* of the patterns of disintegration, in particular the persistent difficulty in defining the goal of integration and the EU sense of purpose. I argue that the birth of the process of integration in Europe is not the fruit of European idealism, but the product of the American strategy to contain the Soviet Union and Communism. Truman posed as prerequisite for the Marshal Plan that European states acted in a coordinate way, thereby making the integration of Europe the 'strategic framework' within which the accommodation of national interests of 'victorious' states such as France had to be set. Jean Monnet, the French 'architect' of the European Coal and Steel Community (1951), corresponded to this 'geopolitical constraint' and adapted Mitrany's functionalism in what became known as the 'Monnet method of integration', blending pragmatic considerations and idealist aspirations. I argue that the 'functional approach' to integration, operating at the level of low-politics with the idea to create a *de facto* solidarity from 'concrete achievements', could 'overlay' underlying political conflicts, but not resolve or transcend them.

The third part presents evidence supporting the argument that the end of the Cold War, and of 'Europe' as a strategic necessity, revealed the fragility of the European institutions, triggering the process of European disintegration. Having lost its hetero-determined geopolitical purpose, 'Europe' proved to be politically and culturally too divided to agree on a road map towards a political union. A fatally flawed monetary union, with which Germany paid the price of its reunification, and an undetermined enlargement, which altered the geopolitical nature of the Union, were the substitute of a missing political project.

The crisis of the monetary union and the disintegrative effect of enlargement on the cohesion of the European bloc are analysed in chapter seven and eight. The crisis of the euro is interpreted *in primis* as the failure of the functionalist gamble and its erroneous assumption of a sequential relationship between 'Euro' and 'Europe'; I present the argument that the political union is the prerequisite, not the product of the monetary union. As to the enlargement, I argue that it has irreversibly altered the nature of the Union, rendering the prospect of political union rather remote. I interpret the EU 'imperial' vocation to continuous enlargement, as expressed in the Laeken Declaration, as the sign of the lack of (geo)political vision of the European leadership.

Finally, I briefly discuss the implications of the patterns of disintegration. European states are redrawing their national strategies in the context of an enlarging, and ever more hollow, Union. The emerging order in Europe is characterised by political fragmentation and powerful centrifugal tendencies, with the European institutions becoming increasingly more irrelevant. Member states are paying a lip service to the cause of integration and re-orienting their policies along national lines. I conclude by pointing out that only a radical re-thinking of the nature and finality of the integration process (a new EU design) could in principle prevent a slow, but inevitable process of EU disintegration and decline.

I conclude by touching upon the crucial issue of the identity of

Europe, indicating that the EU has not to invent a post-modern, fuzzy identity, but to re-discover the spirit and identity of the European society. I rely on a pluralistic theoretical framework, nevertheless making wide use of considerations drawn from the realist theory of international relations.

2 From self-congratulation to disintegration

"The EU has procured peace, liberty and prosperity beyond the dreams of even the most optimistic founding fathers".

J. M. Barroso, March 26, 2007

Fiftieth anniversary of the Rome Treaty

AFTER CENTURIES of divisions and two catastrophic civil wars, the introduction of a pan-European currency, the euro, and Eastern enlargement seemed to finally fulfil the hopes of a united, prosperous and peaceful European Union. Millions of citizens celebrated these events as the fulfilment of the Carolingian dream of a politically and culturally united Europe. As the former European Commission President Romano Prodi declared, "in Europe the rule of law has replaced the crude interplay of power and power politics have lost their influence. [...]. By making a success of integration we are demonstrating to the world that it is possible to create a method for peace"[xiii]. Andrew Moravcsik, a well-known scholar in the field of EU study, defined the EU the 'quite superpower', arguing that the EU resolves conflicts and promotes political and economical reforms in its neighbourhood backed by its "economic, financial, legal and military might"[xiv]. Europe's social and political values, he argued, are globally far more attractive than those associated with the US, making EU's world-wide influence destined to grow. As the world's pre-eminent civilian power and second military power, "Europe is and will foreseeable remain the only superpower besides the United States in a bipolar world"[xv]. The sunny optimism of these years was neatly encapsulated in a book published by Mark Leonard, eloquently titled *Why Europe will Run the 21st Century*[xvi]. European's transformative power, combined with the attractiveness of its social market economy, would render Europe a powerful political actor on the globe stage and a model for the nations of the world.

However, the faith of scholars and European political elites in the 'magnificent and progressive fate' (Leopardi) of the EU proved to be largely short-sighted. Centrifugal tendencies in Europe began to emerge in the 1990s after the collapse of the Soviet Union and became fully manifest in the second half of the 2000s, when the global financial crisis exploded. The Iraqi war was a clear, though certainly not the first, signal of the contradiction between the hopes of unity and the reality of an internally divided EU. Of the four big member states, France and Germany fiercely opposed, whilst Italy and Britain supported, the Bush government's decision to invade Iraq[xvii]. One year before entering the EU club, candidate EU countries in the former Communist bloc such as Poland announced their unconditional support for the US foreign policy. "European unity is a joke", complained Javier Solana, the former representative of the EU in the world[xviii]. The war unveiled not only differences, but also deep divergences in the *perception* of strategic priorities between the states of Europe. "The dream of a common Union foreign policy had failed its first serious test"[xix].

In 2004 member states signed in Rome the Constitution of Europe, designed to raise Europe's global profile and streamline the EU decision-making processes[xx]. However, by 2005 the ratification of the constitution had reached an impasse, as the treaty was rejected in popular referenda in France and the Netherlands. As noted by Chalmers, "the Union was faced not with a single recalcitrant State, such as Denmark and Ireland, as with previous amending Treaties. It was instead confronted with a deep divide in which two-thirds of Member States whished to press ahead whilst one-third did not"[xxi]. Few years after the highly symbolic introduction of the common currency, the popular rejection of the Constitution, as well as the uneven road towards the ratification of the Lisbon Treaty, revealed that a latent and growing Euroskepticism had matured parallel to the formal progresses achieved in the (legalistic) integration of Europe.

In 2005, Czech former president Vaclav Havel affirmed: "the European integration project is fortunately a train moving too fast for anyone to stop it"[xxii]. However, a train can run off the rails, especially when the railway tracks are not well designed –or not even completed. *The Economist* famously captured this image in a fulminant cover just before the launch of the single currency: it represented the Eurozone train departing, with the workers still completing the railway lines. Indeed, the image depicts rather accurately the logic of the Community method: concrete achievements should create the conditions for further (political) integration –thereby completing the railway lines. Many *idéologues* in the European Commission bet on the euro as the touchstone of Jean Monnet's esoteric strategy: to proceed from economic integration to political integration. However, the current *structural* crisis of the euro, "the single most dramatic symbol of Europe's ever closer union"[xxiii], indicates that the functionalist 'gamble' tragically failed.

The ferocious popular reactions to the Greek sovereign debt crisis in Germany, the public protests in Athens and Spain against the EU-imposed economic austerity measures and the political paralysis within the E(M)U revealed the *limited* validity of the (neo) functionalist assumptions. As history and political philosophy might have suggested, no monetary union can prosper or even survive without the *substratum* of a pre-existing solidarity between the *peoples* of Europe –a European *political* community. The 'tragedy' of history is that at the beginning of the 2010s Europe is discovering that deep-seated tensions between its nations and ancient mistrust between its peoples have basically remained where they were in 1950s. The idea that the 'appealing projects' of Europe, undertaken *manu Commissionis*, would 'create' a de facto (political) solidarity crushed against the wall of reality.

Top-level officials in the Bureau of Policy Advisers (BEPA), the EU in-house think tank that should help the Commission frame EU political choices in strategic terms, continue to maintain that, despite all, "fostering cooperation" is the prince's path of integration. "The best answer to this crisis, which is also a crisis of confidence, is a renewed commitment of the Commission to work as close as possible to the people and deliver concrete EU policies"[xxiv]. Asked if the crisis of the EU is *in primis* a crisis of public legitimacy of the EU, one senior political adviser replied:

People fairly understandable cannot follow entirely the decision-making mechanisms and thus tend to see Brussels as a bureaucratic labyrinth. That is why Easy Jet is worth more than one thousand pages of EU legislation; indeed, it has been an incredible integrating factor. EU citizens see in their lives the benefits deriving from EU policies. The efforts of the Commission to establish a common and free market made it possible incredibly cheap flights being available for everyone. The free movement of citizens is perhaps codified in rather complicated treaties, but in concrete it means that today one can freely, move, travel and study everywhere in the Union. Young Europeans are free to travel from Milan to Prague, which was unthinkable twenty-years ago[xxv].

It is difficult to imagine a more functionalist idea of Europe. We shall explore this point later; to be sure, the war of words between Greeks and Germans in the past months is there proving that, despite all, flying to Greek islands with Easy Jet, has not prevented Germans to react to the Greek crisis with bewilderment and hostility. In fact, as noted in 1978 by Hans Morgenthau, economic cooperation "is at best likely to leave the problem of international peace where it found it"[xxvi]. The conflicts of power that separate European nations could be transcended only through a shared grand *political* project built on the basis of the acknowledgment of a communality of values, identity and interests. Peoples are not united by material cooperation, which satisfies material needs, but by the immaterial bonds of a common culture and *Weltanschauung*. The sense of community arises "not from the rules and institutions imposed by a political order, [...] rather it is a product of a sense of common culture and identity"[xxvii]. Finally, as to the (functionalist) belief that legitimacy and public loyalty to the EU should emanate from the perception in mass publics of the concrete benefits deriving from the EU institutions, one could quote the lapidary comment of the father of realism: "when mailing a letter to a foreign country, who would think of giving thanks to the Universal Postal Union for the contribution that international agency is making to the operation?"[xxviii].

PART 2

Finding the origin of the EU disintegrative dynamics

IT IS the theoretical assumption of this paper that the disintegrating dynamics threatening the EU are not accidental snags or occasional seatbacks, but the result of the inability of the European leadership to undertake a fundamental *political* reconsideration of the European project after the end of the Cold War[xxix]. The following chapter investigates the origins of the patterns of disintegration, in particular the influence exercised on the development of the European project by the post-war US hegemony and by the 'philosophy of integration' embraced by key integration agents in the 1950s.

3

History: the Strategic Necessity of Europe

THE PERSISTENT DISAGREEMENT among Europeans on the meaning and goal of European integration seems to find its roots in the history of the integration itself. Indeed, the chief and original architects of a 'united Europe' were not Europeans, but Americans: "today's Europe [...] is very much the product of American foreign policy"[xxx]. Fallen into the abyss of the Second World War to never recover quite again, Europe came through the conflict wrecked, both from a material and a political point of view. As Hoffman notes, "Europe did not merely lose power and wealth [...]. Europe, previously the hearth of the international system, the locus of the world organization, the fount of international law, fell under what de Gaulle has called the two hegemonies"[xxxi], the American and the Soviet one.

The role of the US in promoting a form of European integration cannot be emphasized enough. The American leadership shared the conviction that the war had been largely caused by the emergence of incurable economic contrasts between autarkic competing blocs within Europe during the '30[xxxii]. This kind of consideration soon merged with strictly geo-political concerns, especially after the Kennan's 'long telegram' and the change in the US policy towards the Soviet Union. Ultimately, the profound impact that telegram had on the American foreign policy's re-definition led to the "containment" policy, announced on March 12, 1947 by Truman[xxxiii]. The US was afraid that a lack of unity in Europe could lead to Soviet conquest or internal communist subversion. Precisely for this reason, Truman posed as pre-condition of the Marshall Plan that European countries (falling under the US zone of influence) acted in a coordinated way.

As Kennan put it, "in the long run there can be only three possibilities for the future of western and central Europe. One is German domination. Another is Russian domination. The third is a federated Europe"[xxxiv]. Whilst German economic recovery was a pre-condition for the establishment of a liberal and flourishing European economic order, German rearmament became necessary in order to give effectiveness to the containment policy. European integration was the key: "the idea was to rebuild Germany's economic and military capabilities within European and Atlantic institutions"[xxxv].

On April 3, 1949, on the eve of the signing of the Atlantic Alliance Treaty, president Truman invited the foreign ministers of the future NATO's member states to a working dinner at the White House in order to illustrate them the *grand design* of the American foreign policy, and call for their commitment to it. The US was ready to protect Europeans from the present of Stalin and the past of Hitler. However, Europeans had to renounce to important portions of their sovereignty, melt their economies and welcome Germany (Truman used the expression 'German Reich') to their future economic club[xxxvi]. Evidently, the *primum movens* (prime mover or cause) of the integration of Europe was not the idealism of European states, but American foreign policy. Indeed, a dramatic upheaval such as that produced by the Second World War corresponds to what Robert Gilpin calls a "systemic change", in the aftermath of which norms and institutions of government are re-shaped in order to serve the interests of the most powerful or hegemonic States[xxxvii].

Particularly illuminating it is the circumstance that the European integration project, from its inception to recent developments, entirely occurred parallel to and under the shelter of NATO, the institution that can be considered the main instrument of the American hegemony on the European continent[xxxviii]: a benign and, as noted by John Ikenberry, highly constitutionalised hegemony, but still a military alliance, whose hinge and leader is the USA[xxxix].

To be sure, the idea that European countries share a common culture and civilisation, a fundamental common religious and artistic tradition, as well as a common (*polemic*) history, rendered the strategic project of European integration more viable and -as long as supported by the US- effective; in spite of the wars and the nationalistic twists of the early 20th century, the European countries shared an underlying common cultural and historical identity. However, my argument is that the presence of this shared identity and the idea of Europe as a cultural entity represented a *necessary*, but not *sufficient* condition for the European integration process to be launched. The USA was not only "the post-Second World War pacifier of relations between the major European states, but also one of the engine behind the project of European integration"[xl].

The benevolent (and 'situational'[xli]) hegemony of America over Europe entailed that "European powers had no room for

33

manoeuvre in global politics, no say in international security or international money. The politics of Europe became confined […] to economic interdependence and low politics"[xlii]. From the sign of the Treaty of Paris in 1951, the European integration project was thus conducted in the sphere of low politics, as "the high politics of Western world was managed by the United States, a situation that had existed during the Cold War"[xliii]. The European project was firmly embedded within the America order, a situation that corresponds to what Roman strategy called *imperium in imperio*.

4

Functionalism as Philosophy of Integration: Blending Pragmatism and Idealism

THE EUROPEAN PLAYERS ('victorious' France *in primis*) could but accept as a matter of fact the American 'grand design' of Europe. France was not free, as it initially intended, to prevent the reconstruction of Germany economic (and industrial) power; what it did was to 'adjust' its strategy to the mutated geopolitical picture, by putting forward a plan bringing the management of coal and steal under a supranational High Authority. Jean Monnet, the French former *Commissaire general du Plan de Modernisation et d'Equipement*, was the first to see "that it was in the French *national interest* to draw Germany into an embrace that could allow France to become the first among the Europeans and balance the American dominance. Equally, Germany accepted that the only way to regain respectability and sovereignty was to become deeply integrated in a Western Europe while holding on to America"[xliv]. In other words, if the US needed a cohesive Europe to contain the Soviet Union, France used Europe to contain Germany.

By accommodating this variegated set of interests, the French 'executive architect' of the European Coal and Steal Community, Jean Monnet, found in the functionalist theory a promising ideological support. Mitrany's functional strategy for peace, developed in the 1940s, was to link nations up "by what unites, not by what divides"[xlv], using the material needs cutting across national boundaries as a 'channel for unity'[xlvi]. His functionalist logic was aimed at "overlay political divisions with a spreading web of international activities and agencies, in which and through which the interests and life of all the nations would be gradually integrated"[xlvii]. The concept of 'quasi-autonomous development' of functional schemes or agencies is a crucial component of the functionalist theory of peace: it suggests that, without any formal *plan* being laid down in advance, functional arrangements would *functionally* create 'incentives' for ulterior cooperation[xlviii].

With a "subtle blend of pragmatism and idealism"[xlix], Monnet adapted functionalism to the goal of a united (and peaceful) Europe; in other words, the philosophy of functionalism was put at the service of European federalism. Intellectually, the operation made sense: indeed, European states not only shared common material needs, but also a latent common culture. The functional approach could be used to mask the contradictions of post-war Europe, divided by political rivalries and entangled in geopolitical constraints. Besides, given the political impracticability of any European grand political project (as demonstrated by the failure of the European Defence Community in 1954), functionalism presented the promising perspective to gradually unite Europe starting from material cooperation. To be sure, Monet, although driven by the immediate goal to preserve France's national interest, was a fervent European federalist, as it emerges by the reading of his *Memoirs*. Functionalism became thus the logic of the

Community (or Monnet) method of integration. Robert Shuman, the French Foreign Minister, whose homonymous declaration is virtually unanimously viewed as the *Magna Charta* of the European integration project, famously declared in 1950: "Europe will not be made all at once, or according to a single plan. It will be built through concrete achievements which first create a *de facto* solidarity"[l]. However, as history had to demonstrate, the functional integration of Europe could 'overlay' political divisions, but not *transcend* them. Besides, its elitism and its technocratic nature created the conditions for a structural problem of democratic 'illegitimacy' of the European institutions. As noted by Altiero Spinelli, the Monnet method, depoliticising issues and operating at the level of low-politics, made the first step "easier to obtain", but the later steps "much more difficult to achieve"[li]. Finally, the functional approach to integration was structurally and philosophically flawed: its greatest weakness is the "disaggregation of policymaking, with 'technical experts' negotiating on separate dossiers without taking the broader political context into account"[lii]. This became evident with the end of the Cold War and the consequent change of US attitude towards Europe.

PART 3

THE EU OR THE TRIUMPH OF SUBSTANCIAL VACUITY

5

The End of the Cold War and the Beginning of the Disintegration of Europe

IF THE END of the Soviet Union represented for the US the 'end of history', the new strategic landscape represented for Europe the beginning of politics. The end of the Cold War offered to European leaders the possibility of a fundamental *political* revision of the integration project, which was launched in 1951 under severe geopolitical constraints. During the Cold War, the US, as custodian and guarantor of the political regimes falling upon its sphere of influence, was *de facto* the depositary of decisions about 'peace and war' (or high-politics) for Western Europe. As the former foreign minister of France, Hubert Védrine, put it, "the post-war is Western, not European"[liii].

The end of the Cold War entailed the 'exhaustion' of the West as strategic necessity. 'Europe' ceased to serve the purpose of containing the Soviet Union. The integration of Europe could finally depart from the low road of low-politics, enter the royal path of political integration and realise the 'ever closer Union' prospected in the Treaty of Rome (1957). My argument is that this 'qualitative step forward' did not happen. On the contrary, the end of the cold War coincided with the beginning of the process of European disintegration. Indeed, as explained, the US was the main engine (*primum movens*, paraphrasing Aristotle's metaphysics) behind the integration of Europe; when the US, following the collapse of the Soviet Union, shut down the propulsive engine of integration, the European project discovered to be naked and hidebound: as noted by historian Tony Judt, the European edifice proved to be "fundamentally hollow"[liv]. European leaders were "completely unprepared" to the encounter with history (or high politics) and unable to fully realise all the implications of the end of the Cold War[lv]. The collapse of the Soviet Union revealed thus the total fragility of the European project and of its institutions "as well as its dependency on American leadership".[lvi]

After the Cold War, "the logic of power that linked tight German-France relations, with a positive view of integration from Washington, was fundamentally altered"[lvii]. The US government "was less likely to see a united Europe as a positive, and therefore it was no longer necessary to push the close integration of France and Germany in order to ensure a maximum of anti-Soviet consolidation"[lviii]. Indeed, the United States has been reluctant (to say it with an euphemism) to accept any European project of military and political integration *unbound* from the Atlantic Pact even *after* the end of Cold War. America had no intention to lose the monopoly in the field of Western security exercised through NATO. As the first president Bush's national security adviser, General Brent Scowcroft, explained, "at the end of the cold war the US had found itself in a position of unchallenged power"[lix]. The US foreign policy was designed consequently: the priority was, of course, to maintain the status quo and prevent any major shift in the distribution of power. Europe's political aspiration had to be kept at a minimum, focusing instead on economic growth and commerce. To be sure, both the Clinton and the Bush junior administrations perceived any move towards political integration as a challenge to the American institutional order: when the EU tried to develop its independent defence structure, in the aftermath of the St. Malo Agreement between Britain and France, "the United States' reaction was to accuse Europeans of duplication, discrimination and decoupling. When the EU proved undeterred and continued by its Rapid Reaction Force project, the United States responded by its own 'duplicating' move: a NATO Rapid Reaction Force"[lx]. It goes without saying that the American 'reluctance' put the European integration project "under pressure" and confronted the EU leaders and single states with a "double loyalty dilemma"[lxi].

Without the American leadership, the community method was structurally unable to be the new propulsive engine of integration, or the 'unifying factor'. Despite the hopes of many European functional-federalists, the functional approach to integration did not transcend the post-war unresolved political knots between member states: indeed, as realism suggests, there is no sequential relationship between economic cooperation and political integration. The fall of the Berlin Wall revealed that, in spite of decades of 'concrete achievements' and 'integration', disputes between European states remained where they where in 1951; the fall unfroze *divergent* national interests and "an *unresolved mutual distrust* amongst the members of the Community, but particularly directed against Germany"[lxii]. In the 1990s, a persistent German phobia and the fear of a 'Great Germany' remained the dominant characteristic of European relationships, as well as the real (and flawed) engine of 'integration'[lxiii]: to be sure, Germans discovered in 1989 that European leaders did not want the German unity. Indeed, the prospect of the unification of Germany awaked old nightmares and fears in Europe. President Mitterrand of France and Prime Minister Thatcher of Britain, "unable to hide their horror at the thought of German unification", did their best to find a common strategy to avoid it[lxiv]. When it was clear that the process of unification could not be stopped, also because backed by the American leadership, the (French) solution, once again, was to 'Europeanise' Germany: "it was the shock of German unification and the consequent threat of imbalance within the Franco-German relationship that gave urgency to the EMU negotiation"[lxv]. In other words, the Euro was not the product of disinterested Europeanism, but the result of a political *entente*, signed in 1989 between Helmut Kohl and François Mitterrand[lxvi].

To conclude the chapter, the end of 'Europe' as a strategic necessity trigger the beginning of the disintegrating process of Europe after 1989, which became fully evident in the late 2000s. The Monnet method of integration, if anything, hampered the development of a political approach to integration. The process was launched 'in the hope' that (material) integration would have produced the political consensus to sustain, one day, a political community. Thus the development of the integration process was largely left to lawyers and legal experts, who dominated the debated in the 1960s and 1970s[lxvii]. As Weiler highlighted, the process of integration was 'judicially driven', not politically guided[lxviii]. However, cooperation is not a historical necessity, but a political choice. As lucidly noted by Milward, "interdependence can be rejected by an act of political will"[lxix]: it is an ahistorical simplification to believe that the economic benefits which the EU bring to its constituent parts "can overcome the nationalistic forces of political disintegration within it"[lxx].

6

Patterns of Disintegration Unveiled

IN THE ABSENCE of a European *road map*, the fall of the Berlin Wall and the German reunification determined a strategic and identity crisis of Europe, which European leadership tried to resolve by deepening economic integration[lxxi]. The commission endorsed the vision of a Union "concentrating on the realisation of a few major projects with widespread appeal"[lxxii]. As noted by Weiler, it is hard to recall "a more functionalistic and impoverished conception and self-understanding of Europe"[lxxiii]. Member states proved to have divergent national interests and to disagree on the finality of European integration. What emerged was "a tendency to fall back on narrow interests and a sectorial interpretations of events"[lxxiv]. According to a former chief adviser to the European Commission, despite the change of name from Community to Union, the post-Maastricht project did not make a "convincing entry" into high politics: "the Heads of State and Government preferred to go for a 'traditional' deepening of the project by monetary unification in the hope that the Union would thereby be sufficiently strengthen for a widening of the membership" [lxxv]. A tragically flawed monetary union and an undefined enlargement were the surrogate of a (missing) political project.

7

Monetary (dis)union

THE FUNCTIONAL APPROACH to integration predicted a sequential relationship between Euro and Europe. In 2002, the European Commission's president, Romano Prodi, explained the meaning of the introduction of the euro by saying: "it is not economic at all. It is a completely political step. [...] The euro is just an antipasto"[lxxvi]. Unfortunately, history has proved that the euro easily turned into the antipasto of disintegration, as the monetary union proved unable to functionally create its pre-requisites, that is, a political union or a form of solidarity underpinning it. The sovereign debt crisis of some European states highlighted the 'political unsustainability' of monetary union (EMU), unveiling the "geopolitical bluff codified in the Maastricht Treaty"[lxxvii].

The EMU not only was the price that Germany paid to Europe for its reunification; it was also "a tragically incomplete achievement"[lxxviii], for it was launched in the absence of the necessary political pre-requisites for it to work smoothly, particularly in presence of asymmetric shocks. Clearly, politics was kept out of the monetary union, as demonstrated by its 'intellectually and politically schizophrenic' system of governance: a European Central Bank (ECB) controls monetary policy, but member government still control fiscal policy[lxxix]. Ironically, the great economic and financial disparity amongst EMU countries would have required an even greater political willingness to set up transnational equalization mechanisms based on the fundamental principle of fiscal federalism, whereby a part of the fiscal resources in the best-performing EU countries is transferred to the EU countries in the opposite condition. In fact, this mechanism could in principle avoid differences between economies become big enough to jeopardize the stability and cohesion of the monetary union.

As noted by a plethora of commentators, the political commitment to the euro may be strong enough to bail out excessive debtors, but it may not be so strong to support a closer fiscal integration[lxxx]. Besides, financial tampons can cure the symptoms, but "the underlying contradiction will still be there. And the supply of fudge is not inexhaustible"[lxxxi]. A monetary union should be able to adapt to asymmetric economic cycles "either through labour movement from states in recession to state in high growth, or through reduction in wages and labour costs in states in recession (to attract capital investment)"[lxxxii]. The European Central Bank's restrictive monetary policy and the Stability and Growth Pact limiting public deficit force national government into "Draconian labour market and social welfare reforms"[lxxxiii]. However, as lucidly noted *before* the launch of the euro by McKey, the EU (or EMU) lacks the public legitimacy to impose these reforms. As the Greek crisis clearly illustrates, a supranational, not elected body "is identified as responsible for obliging governments to reduce social benefits in order to loosen the labour market and cut spending"[lxxxiv]. And "government actions lacking legitimacy can result in the breakdown of public order and eventually in revolution and regime change" [lxxxv]. The 2010 deadly riots and the political disturbance in Athens and Madrid illustrate the theory.

Historical examples indicate that reforms of welfare regimes and labour market, like in Britain in the 1980s, have always been legitimised by parties with powerful national appeal: political legitimacy of leaders such as Thatcher has been a crucial component in all these reforms attempts. "External forces -such as a perception of declining international competitiveness- may have played some part in persuading parties in government to cut social spending, but in no case was the discipline imposed by international institutions" [lxxxvi]. In the case of EMU, major supply side reforms, including the loosening of labour markets, are being induced "by a *political* authority lacking *political* legitimacy" [lxxxvii].

To be sure, Euro-stability related concerns are leading to intense pressures on the 'central government' (Brussels) to play a major role in stabilisation and equalisation. However, there is not public legitimacy for any degree of fiscal union and no sense of solidarity that would support 'burden-sharing' within EMU. As recent history indicates, "the public reaction in Germany to the Greek crisis was one of bewilderment and hostility. The press was vociferous in its condemnation: the Greek government should sell its islands or the Acropolis to help funs its debt" [lxxxviii].

In both scenarios, EU-imposed domestic reforms and move towards a fiscal union, the structural underlying problem is the absence of a political union and the lack of public legitimacy of EU's exercise of power. Indeed, "large scale redistribution operated by a central or federal government can only occur if political union accompanies economic union" [lxxxix]. Any move towards fiscal centralization would take place "in the absence of the political connective tissue' engendered by EU-wide parties.

Instead, national parties would be obliged to 'blame' the EU and its institution, including the ECB, for the reforms"[xc]. As the public reaction in Germany to Greek sovereign debt crisis indicates, "little justification in terms of shared beliefs and values" would underpin fiscal redistribution within EMU countries[xci].

Today the Eurozone emperor is naked: "the functionalist gamble has failed"[xcii]. The monetary union not only is not creating the *de facto* solidarity for further political integration, but it is breaking into pieces and unveiling deep-seated feelings of (ethno-monetary) hostility between the peoples of Europe. After all, the Euro was born out of a diffuse German phobia, not exactly a fraternal feeling. The absence of a *political* project behind the monetary union is reflected not only in its system of governance: it is emblematically unveiled in its bills. They do not represent (true) fathers of Europe (Dante, Shakespeare, Leonardo, Goethe, Voltaire, Nietzsche…), but inexistent arches, bridges and doors "as if our continent were no more than a transit point"[xciii]. One can but conclude that the EU remains a desperately abstract construction, or the triumph of "substantial vacuity"[xciv]. Hegel famously wrote that what is real is rational; continuing along this line of reasoning, one could say that the reality of a *crumbling* EMU is the mistaken idea of (European) integration that, in its realisation, is proving its own mistakenness. The Euro crisis is thus, to quote *Der Spiegel*, "plötzlich und erwartet"[xcv]: sudden, but by no means *unexpected*. Instead of unite Europeans, a technocratic approach to integration froze (and perhaps reinforced) the deep cultural, political and monetary differences that divide them. In conjunction with enlargement, euro might well be not the seed of further integration, but the end of the dream of political integration. Today's Germany is proving increasingly unwilling to bail out the 'club Med', corresponding to the catholic South, to save a politically inexistent Europe. Having achieved its reunification, and in the context of profound changes on the global stage, Germany is quickly reconsidering its strategic priorities -and Europe is not on the top of the list.

8

Enlargement and political (dis)union

ONE OF THE PARADOXES of the last years resides in the fact that the integration of the *European Union* occurred parallel to the fragmentation of *Europe*. It suffices to spread an historical atlas before one's eyes to observe that in the last decades -the same years of the European integration and enlargement- the emergence of an 'ever closer union' has been largely offset by the emergence of new ever-smaller *nations* in Europe. Paradigmatic it is the recent destiny of former Yugoslavia, under way of shattering for almost two decades, a process that gave birth to pseudo-nation states such as Bosnia, *de facto* split between Serbs, Muslim and Croats, Montenegro or Kosovo, allegedly a semi-protectorate of mafias[xcvi]. Indeed, the processes of regional and subnational fragmentation in the 'back yard of Europe' (the Balkans) took place under the blessing and the auspices of new nationalisms - and the immobility of the EU. The phenomenon is today described by the term 'Balkanisation', indicating the 'pulsion' to carve out 'national houses', and thus 'even-smaller states', in the name of ethnic purity, arguably not truly the greatest achievement of European civilisation. However, the EU response to the *de facto* fragmentation of the geopolitical landscape in the Balkans has been the development of an inclusive strategy: the legal recognition of the new states' sovereignty was accompanied by the prospect of EU membership (offered, *inter alios*, to Bosnia, Serbia, Montenegro, Kosovo…)[xcvii].

The contradiction between the ethnical-nationalistic character of the new states and the supra-national 'spirit' of the Union is not at odds with the Commission's strategy, as it is perfectly consistent with the functionalist concept of integration. According to the father of functionalism, Mitrany, "the emergence of so many new national States might even be put into the service of international unification. If they are to achieve a promising social foundation for their political independence they need many things in the way of material and technical help and service which are beyond their means and experience; […] such needs should be used deliberately and insistently to set up lines for joint international action"[xcviii]. The functionalist approach to integration is clearly detectable in the European commission's insistence that "enlargement encourage aspirant countries to work together with the EU in realising *common objectives*"[xcix]. However, the Commission's enlargement policy remains highly debatable in its philosophical assumptions, as it not at all clear how some true unity could result out of growing divisions along nationalistic lines in Europe.

However, enlargement reflected not only current thinking in the commission, but was actively supported by the US and its closest ally, Britain, to prevent the emergence of a cohesive European Union. "Enlargement will extend Europe's area of peace, democracy and prosperity"[c], affirmed Blair. However, enlargement entailed a watering down of the Franco-German core, the vertebral column of the European (political) project. It is highly debatable that enlargement was the sole strategy to pacify, democratise and stabilise the turbulent *Eastern* limes. As noted by Jan Zielonka, "the Eastern European 'return to (the) Europe' of democratic and prosperous states is one thing; EU membership is another"[ci]. President Mitterrand of France, for instance, proposed an alternative solution to enlargement and fully-fledged membership, a European Confederation, which *de facto* would have achieved the same objectives without jeopardise the consolidation of the emerging European political community. Indeed, successive rounds of enlargement have increased the cultural, economic, political and social heterogeneity of the EU bloc. As the EU embraced a growing number of actors, histories, ambitions and projects, the possibility to create a European political community became increasingly remote.

Thus, enlargement, rather than favoring the integration of Europe, might on the contrary have severely threatened it; in particular, it might have prevented the consolidation of an emerging European political community[cii]. Two big-bang enlargement rounds in 2004 and 2007 have "obviously made it more difficult for the Union to acquire a centrally governed, let alone a single foreign policy"[ciii]. The new Central Eastern member states are very jealous of their newly reacquired sovereignty and, as declared by Vaclav Klaus, have no intention at all "to dissolve their identity in the EU as a lump of sugar in a cup of coffee"[civ]; they tend to be Atlanticist (as also demonstrated by their unconditional support of the US during the Second Golf War)[cv], and their attitudes towards Russia substantially diverge from that of Germany or France.

The internal heterogeneity of a Union stretching from the Black Sea to the Atlantic Ocean, comprising different histories, projects and ambitions, is fully reflected in today's divergences in the definition of the geo-strategic priorities between EU 27 member states. In this respect, "enlargement transformed the Union – irreversibly as well as dramatically"[cvi]. It altered the geopolitical nature of the bloc, which today is hardly more than 'a temple without altar' (Hegel). Since the collapse of the Berlin wall, the European leadership has explicitly linked the definition of integration to the process of enlargement. The EU considers enlargement as a "key step" towards a closer integration, contributing "to stability in Europe and to the security and well-being of its citizens"[cvii].

However, since the EU has never clearly defined the meaning of integration, appealing to the enlargement to define integration is a *petitio principi*. Indeed, no serious debate about the nature (*finality*) and limits (con-*fines*) of European integration took place. The triumph of neoliberal consensus and the functional, technocratic approach to integration and enlargement dried up the philosophical, cultural and political debate about European identity and Europe's borders. The result is that today's EU is growing and stretching towards east and south and north with no shared and clear ideas about it own meaning, its goals and its scope; in one word, with no idea as to its *telos*.

"Europe is dying from its success: everyone wants to join it at a time when it has doubts about its mission".[cviii] The Preamble to the Laeken declaration, November 2001, eloquently reads: "The only boundary that the European Union draws is defined by democratic and human rights". No declaration could better convey the essence of today's EU: the lack of a *political project* and the absence of a *visionary European leadership*. As observed by Bruckner, "on that principle, India, South Africa, Senegal, Ghana, Canada, Australia, New Zealand, the United States, Japan, South Korea, and a good part of Latin America would be candidate for admission to the European Union"[cix]. Tony Judt masterfully noted: "If we look to European Union as a catch-all solution, chanting 'Europe' like a mantra and waving the banners of 'Europe' in the face of recalcitrant 'nationalist' heretics, we may wake up one day to find that far from solving the problems of our continent, the myth of 'Europe' has become an impediment to recognizing them. ...as though the mere invocation of a united Europe could substitute for solving problems and crises in the present"[cx].

9

The emerging European Order

THE FUNDAMENTAL THESIS presented in this essay is that the disintegrative tendencies of the EU are structurally determined. Their origin can be found in the *extra-European* origin of the European integration process, as well as in the flawed 'functional' method of integration and in the historical reasons why that method was adopted. I have argued that when 'liberated' from its hetero-determined strategic identity (with the end of the Cold War), Europe proved unable to develop an autonomous political project. During the confrontation with the Soviet Union, the US policy towards Europe 'forced' Western European nations to cooperate, and integration became the strategic framework within which European states accommodated their respective national interests. American leadership, and not the functional logic of integration, guaranteed the cohesion of the

European bloc during the Cold War. The declining US support for integration following the collapse of the Soviet Union left the project without leadership, revealing unresolved internal divisions within the bloc. In other words, 1989 dissolved the ambiguity: Europe was not able to enter high politics not only because it was under American tutelage, but also because European states did not agree on the political finality of integration from the very inception of the project, as emblematically revealed by the failure to launch a quintessentially political union (the European Defence Community) in 1954.

As briefly indicated, after the fall of the Berlin Wall, Europeans showed to have no urgency to embrace one another. On the contrary, 1989 spread *Angst* (panic) in the Western European chancelleries before the danger of a 'Great Germany'. Mitterrand, Thatcher and Andreotti shared the 'phobia' (fear) that the *Bundesrepublick* could assume a dominant, hegemonic position in Europe, and Germany paid its reunification by means of the renunciation to its strategic asset, the Mark. The Euro is so little the product of 'Europeanism' that the contrary is actually true: Europeanism was and remains the mask nation-states use to better protect their respective interests and their own (residual) sovereignty.

The other 'great achievement' of integration, namely enlargement, represented an ulterior loss of cohesion and had a "disintegrative impact"[cxi] on the EU. Indeed, it masked the disintegration of the political 'ever closer union' and marked the end of 'Europe' as a political project. Failed on hemi-continental scale, the birth of a European (geo) political actor proved to be even more improbable on pan-continental scale[cxii]. As explained by Paul Taylor, "most [new] states joined the EU in order to reinforce themselves as states rather than to lose themselves in some higher entity"[cxiii]. Besides, enlargement prevented the consolidation of the Franco-German Euro core, altering the geopolitical nature of the Union. "Moving from 15 to 27 nations may well be enough to severely threaten any supranational community already developed"[cxiv]. Indeed, the increase in socio-economic heterogeneity "may foster a sense of alienation among the citizens of the EU"[cxv].

The combination of lack of leadership, absence of political legitimacy and the 'imperial' vocation to continuous enlargement is confronting the EU with the serious risk of 'imperial overstretch', "a concept developed by Paul Kennedy in his analysis of the rise and fall of great powers"[cxvi]. In this context of political fragmentation and lack of cohesion, European states are redrawing their national strategies along geographical, historical and political 'convergence or non-convergence lines' within the EU bloc. In particular, Germany and France are rapidly scaling down their commitment to integration. Until reunification and before enlargement, the EU "had served the German purpose of providing a context for recovering sovereignty and becoming a satisfied power"[cxvii]. However, in recent years, "Germany has increasingly seen itself as 'normal'. Having overcome the burden of history, felt it should be able to talk about its *own* interests –as other countries do"[cxviii]. Today, "more than 50 per cent of Germans have little to no faith in the EU, and over 70 per cent do not see Europe as the future of Germany"[cxix]. Enlargement resulted in Germany redefining its geopolitical space "so that it was centered less on France and Western Europe and more on Central Europe in an enlarged EU, and in the world"[cxx]. Indeed, German foreign policy is today looking outside Europe: Germany's relations with BRIC states "are intensifying", to the extent that some Europeans now fear that "Berlin sees its future with the BRICs rather than with Brussels"[cxxi]. In particular, its strategy is characterised by the special economic relationship with China and by the not-only-energetic synergy with Russia. The privileged relationship with Russia was reflected in Berlin's decision to politically distance itself from Britain and France during the Libya 'crisis'.

France is finding its place in the changing power hierarchy after the Cold War. Mitterrand, Chirac and Sarkozy continued to redraw France's strategies within the ever-enlarging EU, a process that Mitterrand was not able to stop. "Enlargement represented a defeat for the Franco-German strategy linking German unification with a deepening of European integration"[cxxii]: indeed, one explanation of the Constitution's failure to gain approval in France was "the perception that it was a dilution of what had been achieved: it had the character of a last act, a summation, rather than of a new start"[cxxiii]. In this context, France is increasingly acting autonomously, taking the initiative and building 'coalitions' within the EU and using the European banner to promote its interests, especially in the Mediterranean.

In the context of an increasingly powerful Germany, Britain is rediscovering its historical balancing abilities. The Anglo-French axis was clearly operating in the case of the joint 'enforcing' intervention in Libya. There are sound reasons to believe that the humanitarian rationale of the intervention was hardly more than an ideological façade: the two former colonial powers were pursuing their *national* geopolitical and energetic interests in Libya, in the name of Europe and under the European flag of humanitarian aid. Germany, which is energetically dependent on Russia's gas, abstained from supporting the UN resolution. Conversely, France and Britain, which had lively interests in improving their position in Libya (at the expense of Italy), took the occasion to intervene. Italy, *more solito*, tried to guess where the wind of history was blowing and joined the two powers, in the hope not to be excluded from future gas concessions[cxxiv].

The failure to put the common interest of the EU above these particular interests clearly indicates that Europe at the beginning of the 2011s is legally more united, but *de facto* deeply divided. As noted by Erik Holm, "what we see is the confrontation between union and nation, between a European structure lacking the dimension of high politics and divergent national interests"[cxxv]. Centrifugal tendencies are progressively emptying the EU institutions of all meaning. The crisis of the euro revealed the lack of solidarity between the peoples of Europe, feeding "rising nationalism, angst over immigration and simmering distrust between rich and less affluent countries"[cxxvi]. The patterns of disintegration, from economic policy to foreign policy, are today fully manifest and are threatening the survival itself of the EU. At this point, a simple question arises: will the crumbling EU edifice share, soon or later, the fate of the Soviet Union? And were the EU able to safely overcome the present tempest, will the Union be(come) hardly more than a high authority for the management of the single market? In that case, in an international system shifted from an imperfect unipolarism to an asymmetric multipolarism condition (especially following the wear of the American power in the Middle East theatres and the emergence of regional or multiregional powers[cxxvii]), will it be possible for a divided, weak and politically heterogeneous 'Europe' to represent an autonomous pole of the international system? Perhaps, solely the emergence of a new visionary leadership might prevent the decline of Europe, with the development of a truly political project envisaging an inner and homogeneous circle within an ever-looser, ever-enlarging Union (what Germans call *Kerneuropa* or Eurocore).

10

On the European Society and the identity of the EU

Endless invention, endless experiment,

Brings knowledge of motion, but not of stillness;

Knowledge of speech, but not of silence;

All our knowledge brings us nearer to our ignorance,

Where is the Life we have lost in living?

Where is the wisdom we have lost in knowledge?

Where is the knowledge we have lost in information?

- T. S. Eliot, Choruses from "The Rock"

THE DEBATE about the European identity touches upon an issue whose importance cannot be underestimated: the legitimacy of power. The European integration project is empty and likely to collapse without the parallel support of a European identity legitimising and reinforcing it. And this for a very simple reason: the EU exercises, in a limited though effective way, power. EU's market regulations, for instance, affect million of people and have redistributive effects impacting individuals in a number of ways. However, in the absence of a widespread and diffuse acceptance of its authority, EU has little chance to survive, as the exercise of its power, especially when going at detriment of some, will not be perceived as legitimate and therefore rejected. The exercise of *political* power requires and implies the existence of a *polis*, a political community sharing a sense of solidarity and community. Not surprisingly, history indicates that all the attempts to merely exercise power *over* the people without public *legitimacy* have never succeed on the long run. So, is a European identity emerging and are opinion polls underestimating its extension and significance?

The question must be rejected as meaningless, as the EU is already the expression of the existence of an underlying, though fragile, European identity inherited by two millennia of history. The contemporary literature presenting empirical evidence of an emerging European identity as *a consequence* of the establishment of common institutions (namely, the EU) comes always too late, as it inverts the causal and historical direction, taking the effect for the cause. It may well be true the constructivist premise[cxxviii] that the establishment of the European institutions has and had an influence on the behaviour and even the preferences of people, and one can of course try to empirically measure this impact. However, such an investigation is sterile, as far as it remains dumb regarding the *origin* of the European institutions themselves. One could argue that the EU is a State creating its Nation, but this argument forgets the essential: that the European Union is a *Union* created *by* and made *of* nation-states, the greatest majority of which have no intention at all to dissolve their identity in Europe "like a lump of sugar in a cup of coffee"[cxxix]. The parallel between the EU and the creation of 'imaginative communities', namely modern nation-states, is therefore inappropriate, as the European project is aimed neither at replacing the nation-state nor at creating a European super state with the monopoly of the use of the legitimate violence.

My argument, on the contrary, is that the EU as such is *already* the expression and manifestation of an existing and latent European identity. In this sense, opinion polls do not underestimate the *emergence* of a European identity; they tend to neglect the *existence* of a European identity. This identity can and should be promoted, but is not to be created: it constitutes the deep rib and structure of the European building. In its absence, the existence itself of the European Union (of nation-states) could not be explained.

I therefore reject Bruter's distinction between civic and cultural identity[cxxx] as meaningless, for the civic identity, defined as identification with the EU institutions, merely reflects and presupposes a cultural identity, defined as identification with the idea of Europe. I argue that supported by the theoretical framework offered by the English School of International Relations.

Contesting the realist idea, which views international politics as a perpetual state of war of all against all, Hedley Bull introduced the illuminating distinction between a *system of states* and a *society of states* (or international society).

A system of states is formed "when two or more states have sufficient contact between them, and have sufficient impact on one another's decisions, to cause them to behave [...] as a part of a whole"[cxxxi].

A society of states "exists when a group of states, conscious of certain common interests and common values, form a society in the sense that they conceive themselves to be bound by a common set of rules in their relations with one another, and share in the working of *common institutions*"[cxxxii]. In this sense, Persia interacted with the Greek city-states, but was not part of the Greek international society. Turkey and the European states in the XVII, XVIII and XIX century were part of a common international system, making alliances and wars as members of the system, but did not constitute an international society.

An international society is not a state, nor a nation-state. It is a society of states founded upon "a common culture or civilisation, or at least some of the elements of such a civilisation: a common language, a common epistemology and understanding of the universe, a common religion, common ethical code, a common aesthetic or artistic tradition"cxxxiii.

Contrary to the common wisdom and literature, Bull suggested that a 'European society' pre-existed to the evolution of Modern State, both in its dynastic and then national phase, namely in the form of a 'Christian International Society'.

It is a open secret that Christianity, introduced as religion of State in the Roman Empire by Theodosius I in 380 AD, gave Europe its cultural unity: a cultural unity bequeathed to the 'European' continent after the collapse of Rome.

What makes the European Society *European* is an underlying cultural unity, endured throughout all the political and historical upheavals. This cultural continuity and unity, given by the powerful synthesis of the Greek philosophy and Judaism operated by Christianity, is the cradle in which Europe finds its origin and meaning.

The underlying cultural unity and identity of Europe is therefore not a product of Modernity: it was, for sure, not created by the nation-state building-process, at most being true the contrary: the nation states were created on its substratum and could not be created without it.

Actually, the national ideology merely served the purpose to allow the legitimate exercise of power following the decline of the divine conception of legitimacy. Pre-modern monarchs used to justify their power before their subjects through the idea expressed in the formula *omnis potestas a Deo*, all power derives from God. After the American and French Revolution, "the prevailing principle of international legitimacy ceased to be dynastic and became popular"[cxxxiv], shifting the *locus* of legitimacy from God to the people: *omnis potestas a populo*[cxxxv]. However, once the source of power's legitimacy was posed in the people, modern States could successfully affirm themselves only by creating a strong political and social cohesion within certain territorial borders; it was the necessity of 'fusing' individual identity and state interest[cxxxvi] that pushed elites to promote the creation of national narratives (identities) *in* Europe between the XVIII and XIX century[cxxxvii]. It was, in most cases, a pure invention of traditions and 'myths of the origins' reinforced by linguistic standardisation and a public education system inculcating the sense of community and spreading the values of the 'nation', which ultimately "produced one of the most powerful and emotive forms of collective identity in the world"[cxxxviii].

The ideology of nationalism, however, has merely been a device, though a powerful one, "for creating loyalty to a large-scale state"[cxxxix], but has not created the European society nor invented its identity. The origins of the international (European) society are to be found in the early Christian international society: the entire history of *Europe* takes place in these cultural river-bed.

On the contrary, nationalism and the process of collective identification with the symbolic dimension of state power have seriously menaced the existence of the European society, leading to Europe's mass suicide represented by two catastrophic civil wars fought in the name of those 'imaginative communities'[cxl] that are Nations. However, the idea of a European society with common values and interests never disappeared, even during the abysses of the two world wars[cxli].

The awareness of a common civilisation, a common fundamental religion and culture between the European States has sustained the institutions of the European Society well before the establishment of the EU after the Second World War. Amongst these institutions, Bull indicated the international law and diplomacy, as the institution reflecting the idea of ruled and principle-based relations between the European states, and the balance of power, as the institution preserving the existence itself of the international society and system.

As I have tried to indicate, the EU is an institution, perhaps the most promising, of the European society: it expresses the sense of common identity, culture and values shared by its members. An identity forged not simply in the course of centuries, but of millennia and characterised by the cultural revolution engendered by the powerful synthesis of Hellenism and Judaism produced by the Christian religion. Culture is of course continually re-shaped and evolves: however, as far as one recognises a continuum in its evolution, one also recognises its fundamental underlying character beyond all its transformations.

Despite being created upon the rejection of the ideology of identity, the European integration project, having gradually assumed political salience, could not evade the problem of the European identity: "the quest for a people's Europe stems from a belief that the creation of a political community needs the emergence of a 'sense of community'"[cxlii]. Indeed, the legitimacy of power exercised by the EU polity requires the existence of a European political community sharing certain beliefs and values: "willingness to grant the EU authority requires some identification with Europe"[cxliii].

The problem of today's EU lies exactly here: European institutions are persuaded that their task is to *create* a European identity: they do not realise that what they are trying to forge is what lies behind them, supporting and giving meaning to them. The EU has not to invent a post-modern demos and "deliberately construct"[cxliv] the EU around civic and post-modern values, as human rights and the social market economy: the European 'imaginative community' already exists and has been the mortar of the European integration project. The hypothesis is of course that the EU, as an institution giving objectivity to the underlying existence of a European society, has not to *invent* its basis.

I argue that only in presence of a degree of congruence between the public goods provided by the EU and the identity of the European society the European integration process will spark off a virtuous circle in which the society and its institution enjoy reciprocal influence and reinforcement. On the contrary, a European Union that will betray Europeans' trust will also dry up the ideological reserve of trust without which the project is doomed to collapse.

The evolution of this identity in supporting the EU project and in accepting the growing exercise of power by the EU will depend not on the ability of the institutions to invent a open, post-modern and fuzzy identity, but on the *nature* and *quality* of EU public goods and policy outcomes. "An emphasis only on the material benefits of integration will not guarantee continued commitment to the process"[cxlv].

The latent Euro-scepticism is the sign that the reserve of trust for the EU institution, in absence of concrete steps towards a closer conformity with its imaginative community, will not last too long. Citizens' perception of the EU as a 'high authority' more worried about the management of the single market than to the promotion of the interests of the European society does not help. Besides, the policy designed to show that 'Europe exists for the people' and the shift from the conception of them as consumer to citizen clashes with the regulatory nature of today's Europe, with its opaque decision making process and with its prioritisation of economic over political issues. Even a 'common' currency alone means little without the real perception by citizens that the EU is about Europe and not about the market. It is probably true that there is a relationship between the non-emergence, or even a decline, of a strong popular support for the EU and the political ambiguity about the nature and aim of the EU: to the service of citizens or of the economy? Indeed, a convergence of interest between citizens and institutions is required to allow the success of the European project and the emergence of a widespread public legitimacy of the EU exercise of power.

CONCLUSION

Wake-up, Europe!

"Si c'etait à refaire, je commençerais par la culture".

Jean Monnet

WITHOUT AN AWAKENING of the conscience of Europe, promoted by a truly European leadership (itself aware of Europe), the integration project is doomed to fall apart, leaving 'space' to the national ideology, in which the peoples of Europe delude themselves to find their 'identity', cancelled from economic and technological dynamics. However, if one does not go down to the heart of Europe, which pulsates in every European 'nation', such a research of identity will lead to violence, oppression, and abstract construction of identity, thereby betraying again the paradoxical identity of Europe as an endless search for meaning.

If this awakening does not happen soon, Europe is doomed to die of parricide, swallowed up by its most powerful child, *techne*. The European spirit must re-discover its daemon, listen to its original call: remember its fundamental character, and put it back at the core of the project of a finally self-conscious Europe. Without this 'revolution' of values, without this 'change of vision', which at the same time would be sunset of the only-market-Europe, Europe will sink into a deeper sleep. Moreover, a Europe 'united' and legitimised only by the material benefits is a Europe deeply unstable, essentially divided: when such benefits turn into disadvantages, as it is happening with the crisis of the Euro, everything falls apart, everything comes down. The authentic European unity is the underlying unity of its society: a European political identity can be founded only on the ethical community (ethos) of the European spirit; and only on such a political identity can be build an European Union. A "union of projects" is a temple completely empty, lifeless, and if Europe thinks of itself in pragmatic-functional terms, then it is issuing its own voluntary death sentence.

However, the European crisis, as *krisis*, it is also *possibility*: possibility of a European renewal, which can only happen as a spiritual renewal, before being economic and political: awakening of the consciousness and awareness of Europe.

BIBLIOGRAPHY

Aeshimann, Riché (1996). La guerre de sept ans : histoire secrète du franc fort, 1989-1996, Calmann-Lévy

Booker, C., North, R. (2005) The great deception: can the European Union survive?, Continuum

Bull, H. (1977). The anarchical society, Palgrave MacMillan

Bruckner, P. (2010). The Tyranny of Guilt, Princeton

Cacciari, M. (2003). Geo-filosofia dell'Europa, Adelphi

Cacciari, M. (1997). L'arcipelago, Adelphi

Cacciari, M. (1990). Dell'Inizio, Adelphi

Cacciari, M. (2009). Hamletica, Adelphi

Caracciolo, L. (2011). America vs America, Laterza

Chalmers, Davies, Monti (2010): European Union Law, Cambridge

Der Spiegel, Heft 25/2011

Donà, M. (2012). Filosofia dell'errore, Bompiani

Dyson, K. & K. Featherstone (1999). The Road to Maastricht; Chapter 17. Oxford

European Commission (2010). 'Enlargement Strategy and Main Challenges 2010-2011', available at http://ec.europa.eu/enlargement/press_corner/key-documents/reports_nov_2010_en.htm (last accessed 19 August 2011)

Etzioni, A. (2001). Political Unification Revisited: On Building Supranational Communities, Lanham:Lexicon Books

Featherstone, K. (2011). 'The Greek Sovereign Debt Crisis and EMU: A Failing State in a Skewed Regime,' in JCMS 2011 Volume 49. Number 2. pp.193-217

Featherstone, K. (1994). 'Jean Monnet and the 'Democratic Deficit' in the European Union', in JCMS 1994 Volume 32. Number 2. pp.149-170

Gilpin, R. (1981): War and Change in World Politics, Cambridge

Guérot, U., Hénard, J. (2011). What does Germany Think about Europe?, European Council on Foreign Relations

Hass, Ernst. (2006): 'The Uniting of Europe', in Debates on European Integration, Palgrave MacMillan

Hix, S. (2005). 'Economic and Monetary Union' in The Political System of the European Union, 2nd edn, Palgrave.

Heidegger, M. (1994) Nietzsche, Adelphi

Heidegger, M. (2007). Contributi alla filosofia, Adelphi

Hoffmann, Stanley. (2006): 'Obstinate or Obsolete? The Fate of the Nation-State' in: Debates on European Integration: A Reader. Mette Eilstrup-Sangiovanni, Palgrave Macmillan

Holm, E. (2001). The European Anarchy, Copenhagen Business School

Ikenberry, G. John. (2001): After Victory, Princeton University Press

Interview, conducted in Brussels the 17 March 2011

Joffe, Joseph. (1984): 'Europe's American Pacifer', Foreign Policy, 54

Judt, T. (1996). 'Europe: The Grand Illusion', in The New York Review of Books, 11 July 1996

Kissinger, Henry. (1994): Diplomacy, Simon and Schuster Paperbacks

Kurt, U. (2009). 'Europe of Monnet, Schumann and Mitrany: a Historical Glance to the EU from the Functional Perspective', in European Journal of Economic and Political Studies, 2009 Volume 2

Laffan, B. (1996). 'The Politics of Identity and Political Order in Europe', Journal of Common Market Studies, 34(1), 81–102

Leonard, M. (2005). Why Europe will run the 21st Century, Fourth Estate

Letta, E., Caracciolo L. (2010). L'Europa è finita?, Add Editore

Limes, (2011). La Guerra di Libia, l'Espresso

Kagan, Robert. (2003): Paradise&Power, Atlantic Books

Majone, G. (2005). Dilemmas of European Integration, Oxford

Marquand, D. (2011). The End of the West, Princeton

McKay, D. (1999). 'The political sustainability of European Monetary Union' in British Journal of Political Science, vol. 29, no. 3, pp. 463-485

Milward, A. (2000). European Rescue of the Nation State, Routledge

Mitrany, D. (1948). 'The Functional Approach to World Organization', in International Affairs (Royal Institute of International Affairs 1944-), Volume 24, Number 3

Mitrany, D. (2006). 'A Working Peace System: An Argument for the Functional Development of International Organization', in Debates on European Integration: A Reader. Mette Eilstrup-Sangiovanni, Palgrave Macmillan

Moravcsik, A. (2009): 'Europe: The quite superpower', in French Politics 7(3/4), pp. 403-422

Moravcsik, Andrew. (1998) The Choice for Europe, Cornell University Press

Moravcsik, Andrew. (2000): 'De Gaulle Between Grain and Grandeur: The Political Economy of French EC Policy, 1958-1970 (Part 1)'. Journal of Cold War Studies, Vol. 2(2), pp. 3-43

Morgenthau, H. (2006). Politics Among Nations, McGraw Hill

Parsi, Vittorio Emanuele. (2009): 'La vera sfida per l'Europa: da consumatore a produttore di sicurezza', in: L'Europa nel sistema internazionale, Laschi-Telò, il Mulino

Rachman, G. (2011): Zero Sum World, Atlantic Books, London

Risse, T., (2004). 'European Institutions and Identity change: What Have we Learned?' in Herrmann, R., Brewer, M., and Risse, T. Transnational Identities. Lanham: Rowman and Littlefield. Chapter 11, 247-72

Sartori, G. (1987). The theory of democracy revisited, Chatham Publishers

Schumann, R. (1950), Declaration of 9 May 1950, available at http://europa.eu/abc/symbols/9-may/decl_en.htm, last access 19 August

2011

Stürmer, M. (2010). 'La moneta senza storia alla prova della storia', in I quaderni speciali di Limes, April 2010

The Economist, 2nd December 2010, available at http://www.economist.com/node/17627547?story_id=17627547; last access 19 August 2011

Thiesse, A. M. (2001). La creazione delle identità nazionali in Europa, Il Mulino

Time, 22 August 2011

Tyalor, P. (2008). The end of European Integration, Routledge

Védrine, Hubert. (2008): 'Le projet européen: Occident ou Europe d'abord?', in: Notre Europe, Rocard-Gnesotto, Laffont

Vollaard, H. (2008). 'A Theory of European Disintegration', Fourth Pan-European Conference on EU Politics, 25th – 27th September 2008, University of Latvia, Riga, available at: http://www.jhubc.it/ecpr-riga/virtualpaperroom/017.pdf, last access 19 August 2011

Wallace, W. (1994). Regional Integration: The West European Experience, Washington DC: The Brookings Institution.

Weiler, J.H.H. (1994). 'A Quite Revolution', in Comparative Political Studies, Vol. 26 No 4, pp 510-534

Zielonka, Jan. (2006): Europe as Empire, Oxford

NOTES

i (Marquand 2011:109)
ii (Majone 2005:42)
iii (see Holm 2001)
iv (Zielonka 2006:53)
v (Holm 2001:9)
vi (Marquand 2011:154)
vii (Article 3(1) Treaty of the European Union)
viii (Marquand 2011:154)
ix (Vollaard 2008:10)
x (Guérot, Hénard 2011:5)
xi (quoted in Marquand 2011:24)
xii (Taylor 2008)
xiii (quoted in Kagan 2003:60)
xiv (Moravcsik 2009:410)
xv (Ibidem:403)
xvi (Rachman 2010:148)
xvii (Marquand 2011:48)
xviii (Rachman 2010:147)
xix (Marquand 2011:48)
xx (Marquand 2011:45)
xxi (Chalmers et al. 2010:38)
xxii (quoted in Booker, North 2005:540)
xxiii (Rachman 2010:184)
xxiv (Interview)
xxv (Ibidem)
xxvi (Morgenthau 2006:536)
xxvii (Holm 2001:17)
xxviii (Morgenthau 2006:528)
xxix (see Holm 2001)
xxx (Kagan 2003:70)
xxxi (Hoffman 2006:140)

xxxii (Ikenberry 2001:203)
xxxiii (Kissinger 1994:447)
xxxiv (Ikenberry 2001:207)
xxxv (Ibidem: 207)
xxxvi (Stürmer 2010:85)
xxxvii (Gilpin 1981)
xxxviii (Parsi 2009)
xxxix (see Ikenberry 2001)
xl (Zielonka 2006:157)
xli (see Hoffman 2006)
xlii (Holm 2001:66)
xliii (Holm 2001:10)
xliv (Holm 2001: 66 emphasis added)

xlv (Mitrany 1948:359)
xlvi (Ibidem)
xlvii (Mitrany 1943:45)
xlviii (Mitrany 1948)
xlix (Marquand 2011:106)
l (Schumann Declaration, 1950)
li (quoted in Featherstone 1994:165)
lii (Wallace 1994: 75)
liii (Védrin 2008: 280)
liv (Judt 1996:9)
lv (Holm 2001:209)
lvi (Holm 2001:209)
lvii (Taylor 2008:21)
lviii (Taylor 2008:21)
lix (Rachman 2011:176)
lx (Zielonka 2006:158)
lxi (Zielonka 2006:158)
lxii (Holm 2001:209))
lxiii (Caracciolo 2011:40)
lxiv (Holm 2001:211)
lxv (Dyson, Featherstone 1999: 757)
lxvi (see Aeschimann, Riché 1996)
lxvii (see Holm 2001; Taylor 2008)
lxviii (see Weiler 1994)
lxix (Milward 2000:8)
lxx (Ibidem)
lxxi (see Caracciolo, Letta 2010; Holm 2001)
lxxii (quoted in Chalmers et al. 2010:354)
lxxiii (Weiler 2002, quoted in Chalmers et al. 2010:355)
lxxiv (Holm 2001:209)
lxxv (Holm 2001:63)
lxxvi (Interview on CNN 1 January 2002)
lxxvii (Letta, Caracciolo 2010: 30)
lxxviii (Marquand 2011:23)
lxxix (Ibidem)
lxxx (The Ecomomist, 2nd December 2010)
lxxxi (Marquand 2001:49)
lxxxii (Hix 2005:338)
lxxxiii (McKay 1999:473)
lxxxiv (McKey 1999:478)
lxxxv (McKay 1999:485)
lxxxvi (McKey 1999:478)
lxxxvii (Ibidem:479)
lxxxviii (Featherstone 2011:201)
lxxxix (McKay 1999:474)
xc (Ibidem)
xci (Ibidem:479)
xcii (Marquand 2011:50)
xciii (Bruckner 2010: 92)
xciv (Ibidem)

[xcv] (Der Spiegel, 25/2011)
[xcvi] (Caracciolo 2010)
[xcvii] (COMM 2010)
[xcviii] (Mitrany 1944:8)
[xcix] (COMM 2010:3)
[c] (quoted in Booker, North 2005)
[ci] (Zielonka 2006:24)
[cii] (Etzioni 2001:xxxvi)
[ciii] (Zielonka 2006:146)
[civ] (quoted in Zielonka 2006:89
[cv] (see Taylor 2008)
[cvi] (Marquand 2011:151)
[cvii] (Comm 2010)
[cviii] (Bruckner 2010:190)
[cix] (Ibidem:190)
[cx] (Judt 1996:9)
[cxi] (Vollaard 2008:11)
[cxii] (Caracciolo 2011:28)
[cxiii] (Taylor 2008:16)
[cxiv] (Etzioni 2001: xxxvi)
[cxv] (Vollaard 2008:11)
[cxvi] (Vollaard 2008:13)
[cxvii] (Taylor 2008:67)
[cxviii] (Guérot, Hénard 2011:6)
[cxix] (Ibidem)
[cxx] (Taylor 2008:21)
[cxxi] (Ibidem)
[cxxii] (Taylor 2008:21)
[cxxiii] (Taylor 2008:20)
[cxxiv] (LIMES 2011)
[cxxv] (Holm 2001:10)
[cxxvi] (Time, 22 August 2011)
[cxxvii] (Parsi 2009)
[cxxviii] (Risse 2004)
[cxxix] (Klaus 1999)
[cxxx] (Risse 2004)
[cxxxi] (Bull 1977:9)
[cxxxii] (Ibidem:13)
[cxxxiii] (Bull 1977:15)
[cxxxiv] (Ibidem:33)
[cxxxv] (Sartori 1987:28-29)
[cxxxvi] (see Gilpin 1981)
[cxxxvii] (see Thiesse 2001)
[cxxxviii] (Laffan 1996:85)
[cxxxix] (Gilpin 1981: 150)
[cxl] (Anderson 1991:5-7)
[cxli] (see Bull 1977)
[cxlii] (Laffan 1996:96)
[cxliii] (Risse 2004:250)
[cxliv] (Risse 2004:267)

cxlv (Laffan 1996:95)

Interviews carried out at the European Commission in Brussels (March 2011)

www.ingramcontent.com/pod-product-compliance
Lightning Source LLC
Chambersburg PA
CBHW072339290526
45794CB00002B/936